FAVORITE
POEMS
for
CHRISTMAS

A CHILD'S COLLECTION

FOR GRANDMA CLEVELAND

Copyright © 2021 by Bushel & Peck Books.

Published by Bushel & Peck Books, a family-run publishing house in Fresno, California, that believes in uplifting children with the highest standards of art, music, literature, and ideas. Find beautiful books for gifted young minds at www.bushelandpeckbooks.com.

Type set in Temeraire and Baskerville.

Designed by David Miles.

Bushel & Peck Books is dedicated to fighting illiteracy all over the world. For every book we sell, we donate one to a child in need—book for book. To nominate a school or organization to receive free books, please visit www.bushelandpeckbooks.com.

ISBN: 9781638190196

First Edition

Printed in the United States

10 9 8 7 6 5 4 3 2 1

FAVORITE
POEMS
for
CHRISTMAS

A CHILD'S COLLECTION

BUSHEL
& PECK
BOOKS

CONTENTS

CAROL

Excerpt from The Wind in the Willows
by Kenneth Grahame

Villagers all, this frosty tide,
Let your doors swing open wide,
Though wind may follow, and snow beside,
Yet draw us in by your fire to bide;
    Joy shall be yours in the morning!

Here we stand in the cold and the sleet,
Blowing fingers and stamping feet,
Come from far away you to greet—
You by the fire and we in the street—
    Bidding you joy in the morning!

For ere one half of the night was gone,
Sudden a star has led us on,
Raining bliss and benison—
Bliss to-morrow and more anon,
    Joy for every morning!

Goodman Joseph toiled through the snow—
Saw the star o'er a stable low;
Mary she might not further go—
Welcome thatch, and litter below!
    Joy was hers in the morning!

And then they heard the angels tell
"Who were the first to cry NOWELL?
Animals all, as it befell,
In the stable where they did dwell!
    Joy shall be theirs in the morning!"

THE LEAST OF CAROLS

Sophie Jewett

Loveliest dawn of gold and rose
Steals across undrifted snows;
In brown, rustling oak leaves stir
Squirrel, nuthatch, woodpecker;
Brief their matins, but, by noon,
All the sunny wood's a-tune:
Jays, forgetting their harsh cries,
Pipe a spring note, clear and true;
Wheel on angel wings of blue,
Trumpeters of Paradise;
Then the tiniest feathered thing,
All a-flutter, tail and wing,
Gives himself to caroling:

"Chick-a-dee-dee, chick-a-dee!
Jesulino, hail to thee!
Lowliest baby born to-day,

Pillowed on a wisp of hay;
King no less of sky and earth,
    And singing sea;
Jesu! Jesu! most and least!
For the sweetness of thy birth
Every little bird and beast,
Wind and wave and forest tree,
Praises God exceedingly,
    Exceedingly."

IN THE BLEAK MIDWINTER

Christina G. Rossetti

In the bleak mid-winter
  Frosty wind made moan,
Earth stood hard as iron,
  Water like a stone;
Snow had fallen, snow on snow,
  Snow on snow,
In the bleak mid-winter
  Long ago.

Our God, Heaven cannot hold Him
  Nor earth sustain;
Heaven and earth shall flee away
  When He comes to reign.
In the bleak mid-winter
  A stable-place sufficed
The Lord God Almighty
  Jesus Christ.

Angels and archangels
    May have gathered there,
Cherubim and seraphim
    Thronged the air;
But only His Mother
    In her maiden bliss
Worshipped her Beloved
    With a kiss.

What can I give Him,
    Poor as I am?
If I were a shepherd
    I would bring a lamb,
If I were a Wise Man,
    I would do my part,—
Yet what I can I give Him,
    Give my heart.

THE CHRISTMAS SILENCE

Margaret Deland

Hushed are the pigeons cooing low,
    On dusty rafters of the loft;
And mild-eyed oxen, breathing soft,
    Sleep on the fragrant hay below.

Dim shadows in the corner hide;
    The glimmering lantern's rays are shed
Where one young lamb just lifts his head,
    Then huddles 'gainst his mother's side.

Strange silence tingles in the air;
    Through the half-open door a bar
Of light from one low hanging star
    Touches a baby's radiant hair—

No sound—the mother, kneeling, lays
    Her cheek against the little face.

Oh human love! Oh heavenly grace!
    'Tis yet in silence that she prays!

Ages of silence end to-night;
    Then to the long-expectant earth
Glad angels come to greet His birth
    In burst of music, love, and light!

FROM FAR AWAY

William Morris

From far away we come to you.

    The snow in the street, and the wind on the door,

To tell of great tidings, strange and true.

      Minstrels and maids, stand forth on the floor.

        From far away we come to you,

        To tell of great tidings, strange and true.

For as we wandered far and wide,

    The snow in the street, and the wind on the door,

What hap do you deem there should us betide?

      Minstrels and maids, stand forth on the floor.

Under a bent when the night was deep,

    The snow in the street, and the wind on the door,

There lay three shepherds, tending their sheep.

      Minstrels and maids, stand forth on the floor.

"O ye shepherds, what have ye seen,

    The snow in the street, and the wind on the door,

To stay your sorrow and heal your teen?"

 Minstrels and maids, stand forth on the floor.

"In an ox stall this night we saw,

 The snow in the street, and the wind on the door,

A Babe and a maid without a flaw.

 Minstrels and maids, stand forth on the floor.

"There was an old man there beside;

 The snow in the street, and the wind on the door,

His hair was white, and his hood was wide.

 Minstrels and maids, stand forth on the floor.

"And as we gazed this thing upon,

 The snow in the street, and the wind on the door,

Those twain knelt down to the little one.

 Minstrels and maids, stand forth on the floor.

"And a marvellous song we straight did hear,

 The snow in the street, and the wind on the door.

That slew our sorrow and healed our care."

 Minstrels and maids, stand forth on the floor.

News of a fair and marvellous thing,

 The snow in the street, and the wind on the door,

Nowell, Nowell, Nowell, we sing.

 Minstrels and maids, stand forth on the floor.

  From far away we come to you,

  To tell of great tidings, strange and true.

LORDINGS, LISTEN TO OUR LAY

Old Carol

Lordings, listen to our lay—
We have come from far away
    To seek Christmas;
In this mansion we are told
He His yearly feast doth hold:
    'Tis to-day!
May joy come from God above,
To all those who Christmas love.

'TWAS JOLLY, JOLLY WAT

C. W. Stubbs

'Twas jolly, jolly Wat, my foy,
He was a goodman's shepherd boy,
    And he sat by his sheep
    On the hill-side so steep,
    And piped this song,
        Ut hoy! Ut hoy!
    O merry, merry sing for joy,
        Ut hoy!

A'down from Heav'n that is so high
There came an angel companye,
    And on Bethlehem hill
    Thro' the night-tide so still
    Their song out-rang:
        On high, On high,
    O glory be to God on high,
        On high!

Now must Wat go where Christ is born,
Yea, go and come again to-morn.
    And my pipe it shall play,
    All my heart it doth say
    To Shepherd King:
        Ut hoy! Ut hoy!
    O merry, merry sing for joy,
        Ut hoy!

O peace on earth, good will to men,
The angels sang again, again,
    For to you was He born
    On this Christmas morn,
    So sing we all:
        On high, On high,
    O glory be to God on high,
        On high!

Jesu my King, it's naught for Thee,
A bob of cherries, one, two, three,
    But my tar-box and ball,
    And my pipe, I give all
    To Thee, my King.
        Ut hoy! Ut hoy!

O merry, merry sing for joy,
    Ut hoy!

Farewell, herd-boy, saith Mary mild.
Thanks, jolly Wat, smiled Mary's child,
    For fit gift for a king
    Is your heart in the thing.
    So pipe you well,
        For joy, for joy!
    O merry, merry sing for joy,
        Ut hoy!

BOOTS AND SADDLES

Provençal Noël of Nicholas Saboly

———

Our shepherds all
    As pilgrims have departed,
Our shepherds all
    Have gone to Bethlehem.
They gladly go
    For they are all stout-hearted,
They gladly go—
    Ah, could I go with them!

I am too lame to walk,
    Boots and saddles, boots and saddles,
I am too lame to walk,
    Boots and saddles, mount and ride.

A shepherd stout
    Who sang a catamiaulo,

A shepherd stout
Was walking lazily.
He heard me speak
And saw me hobbling after,
He turned and said
He would give help to me.

"Here is my horse
That flies along the high-road,
Here is my horse,
The best in all the towns.
I bought him from
A soldier in the army,
I got my horse
By payment of five crowns."

When I have seen
The Child, the King of Heaven,
When I have seen
The Child who is God's son,
When to the mother,
I my praise have given,
When I have finished,
All I should have done:

No more shall I be lame,

 Boots and saddles, boots and saddles,

No more shall I be lame,

 Boots and saddles, mount and ride.

THE NEIGHBORS OF
BETHLEHEM

Thirteenth Century French Carol

Good neighbor, tell me why that sound,
That noisy tumult rising round,
Awaking all in slumber lying?
Truly disturbing are these cries,
All through the quiet village flying,
O come ye shepherds, wake, arise!
What, neighbor, then do ye not know
God hath appeared on earth below
And now is born in manger lowly!
In humble guise he came this night,
Simple and meek, this infant holy,
Yet how divine in beauty bright.
Good neighbor, I must make amend,
Forthwith to bring Him will I send,
And Joseph with the gentle Mother.
When to my home these three I bring,
Then will it far outshine all other,
A palace fair for greatest king!

CAROL OF THE RUSSIAN CHILDREN

Russian Folk Song

Snow-bound mountains, snow-bound valleys,
Snow-bound plateaus, clad in white,
Fur-robed moujiks, fur-robed nobles,
Fur-robed children, see the light.
Shaggy pony, shaggy oxen,
Gentle shepherds wait the light;
Little Jesus, little Mother,
Good St. Joseph, come this night.

SIGNS OF CHRISTMAS

Edwin Lees

When on the barn's thatch'd roof is seen
The moss in tufts of liveliest green;
When Roger to the wood pile goes,
And, as he turns, his fingers blows;
When all around is cold and drear,
Be sure that Christmas-tide is near.

When up the garden walk in vain
We seek for Flora's lovely train;
When the sweet hawthorn bower is bare,
And bleak and cheerless is the air;
When all seems desolate around,
Christmas advances o'er the ground.

When Tom at eve comes home from plough,
And brings the mistletoe's green bough,
With milk-white berries spotted o'er,

And shakes it the sly maids before,
Then hangs the trophy up on high,
Be sure that Christmas-tide is nigh.

When Hal, the woodman, in his clogs,
Bears home the huge unwieldy logs,
That, hissing on the smouldering fire,
Flame out at last a quiv'ring spire;
When in his hat the holly stands,
Old Christmas musters up his bands.

When cluster'd round the fire at night,
Old William talks of ghost and sprite,
And, as a distant out-house gate
Slams by the wind, they fearful wait,
While some each shadowy nook explore,
Then Christmas pauses at the door.

When Dick comes shiv'ring from the yard,
And says the pond is frozen hard,
While from his hat, all white with snow,
The moisture, trickling, drops below,
While carols sound, the night to cheer,
Then Christmas and his train are here.

CHRISTMAS EVE

John Davidson

In holly hedges starving birds
  Silently mourn the setting year;
Upright like silver-plated swords
  The flags stand in the frozen mere.

The mistletoe we still adore
  Upon the twisted hawthorn grows:
In antique gardens hellebore
  Puts forth its blushing Christmas rose.

Shrivell'd and purple, cheek by jowl,
  The hips and haws hang drearily;
Roll'd in a ball the sulky owl
  Creeps far into his hollow tree.

In abbeys and cathedrals dim
  The birth of Christ is acted o'er;

The kings of Cologne worship him,
    Balthazar, Jasper, Melchior.

The shepherds in the field at night
    Beheld an angel glory-clad.
And shrank away with sore afright.
    "Be not afraid," the angel bade.

"I bring good news to king and clown,
    To you here crouching on the sward;
For there is born in David's town
    A Saviour, which is Christ the Lord.

"Behold the babe is swathed, and laid
    Within a manger." Straight there stood
Beside the angel all arrayed
    A heavenly multitude.

"Glory to God," they sang; "and peace,
    Good pleasure among men."
The wondrous message of release!
    Glory to God again!

Hush! Hark! the waits, far up the street!

    A distant, ghostly charm unfolds,

Of magic music wild and sweet,

    Anemones and clarigolds.

CAROL OF THE BIRDS

Bas-Quercy

Whence comes this rush of wings afar.
Following straight the Noël star?
Birds from the woods in wondrous flight,
Bethlehem seek this Holy Night.
"Tell us, ye birds, why come ye here.
Into this stable, poor and drear?"
"Hast'ning we seek the new-born King,
And all our sweetest music bring."
Hark how the green-finch bears his part,
Philomel, too, with tender heart,
Chants from her leafy dark retreat
Re, mi, fa, sol, in accents sweet.
Angels and shepherds, birds of the sky,
Come where the Son of God doth lie;
Christ on the earth with man doth dwell.
Join in the shout, Noël, Noël.

THE SHEPHERDS HAD AN ANGEL

Christina G. Rossetti

The shepherds had an angel,
　　The wise men had a star;
But what have I, a little child,
　　To guide me home from far,
Where glad stars sing together,
　　And singing angels are?

Lord Jesus is my Guardian,
　　So I can nothing lack;
The lambs lie in His bosom
　　Along life's dangerous track:
The wilful lambs that go astray
　　He, bleeding, brings them back.

Those shepherds thro' the lonely night
　　Sat watching by their sheep,

Until they saw the heav'nly host
    Who neither tire nor sleep,
All singing Glory, glory,
    In festival they keep.

Christ watches me, His little lamb,
    Cares for me day and night,
That I may be His own in heav'n;
    So angels clad in white
Shall sing their Glory, glory,
    For my sake in the height.

Lord, bring me nearer day by day,
    Till I my voice unite,
And sing my Glory, glory,
    With angels clad in white.
All Glory, glory, giv'n to Thee,
    Thro' all the heav'nly height.

SONG OF A SHEPHERD
BOY AT BETHLEHEM

Josephine Preston Peabody

Sleep, Thou little Child of Mary,
    Rest Thee now.
Though these hands be rough from shearing
    And the plow,
Yet they shall not ever fail Thee,
When the waiting nations hail Thee,
Bringing palms unto their King.
    Now—I sing.

Sleep, Thou little Child of Mary,
    Hope divine.
If Thou wilt but smile upon me,
    I will twine
Blossoms for Thy garlanding.
Thou'rt so little to be King,
    God's Desire!

Not a brier
Shall be left to grieve Thy brow;
Rest Thee now.

Sleep, Thou little Child of Mary,
Some fair day
Wilt Thou, as Thou wert a brother,
Come away
Over hills and over hollow?
All the lambs will up and follow.
Follow but for love of Thee.
Lov'st Thou me?

Sleep, Thou little Child of Mary,
Rest Thee now.
I that watch am come from sheep-stead
And from plough.
Thou wilt have disdain of me
When Thou'rt lifted, royally,
Very high for all to see:
Smilest Thou?

THE HALLOWED TIME

Shakespeare

Some say that ever 'gainst that season comes
Wherein our Saviour's birth is celebrated,
The bird of dawning singeth all night long;
And then, they say, no spirit dares stir abroad;
The nights are wholesome, then no planets strike,
No fairy takes, nor witch hath power to charm,
So hallowed and so gracious is the time.

THE SHEPHERD WHO STAYED

Theodosia Garrison

There are in Paradise
Souls neither great nor wise,
Yet souls who wear no less
The crown of faithfulness.

My master bade me watch the flock by night;
My duty was to stay. I do not know
What thing my comrades saw in that great light,
I did not heed the words that bade them go,
I know not were they maddened or afraid;
       I only know I stayed.

The hillside seemed on fire; I felt the sweep
Of wings above my head; I ran to see
If any danger threatened these my sheep.
What though I found them folded quietly,

What though my brother wept and plucked my sleeve,
        They were not mine to leave.

Thieves in the wood and wolves upon the hill,
My duty was to stay. Strange though it be,
I had no thought to hold my mates, no will
To bid them wait and keep the watch with me.
I had not heard that summons they obeyed;
        I only know I stayed.

Perchance they will return upon the dawn
With word of Bethlehem and why they went.
I only know that watching here alone,
I know a strange content.
I have not failed that trust upon me laid;
        I ask no more—I stayed.

THE OXEN

Thomas Hardy

Christmas Eve, and twelve of the clock.
　"Now they are all on their knees,"
An elder said as we sat in a flock
　By the embers in hearthside ease.

We pictured the meek mild creatures where
　They dwelt in their strawy pen,
Nor did it occur to one of us there
　To doubt they were kneeling then.

So fair a fancy few would weave
　In these years! Yet, I feel,
If someone said on Christmas Eve,
　"Come; see the oxen kneel

"In the lonely barton by yonder coomb
  Our childhood used to know,"
I should go with him in the gloom,
  Hoping it might be so.

ON THE MORNING OF CHRIST'S NATIVITY

John Milton

I

This is the Month, and this the happy morn
Wherin the Son of Heav'ns eternal King,
Of wedded Maid, and Virgin Mother born,
Our great redemption from above did bring;
For so the holy sages once did sing,
That he our deadly forfeit should release,
And with his Father work us a perpetual peace.

II

That glorious Form, that Light unsufferable,
And that far-beaming blaze of Majesty,
Wherwith he wont at Heav'ns high Councel-Table,

To sit the midst of Trinal Unity,

He laid aside; and here with us to be,

Forsook the Courts of everlasting Day,

And chose with us a darksom House of mortal Clay.

III

Say Heav'nly Muse, shall not thy sacred vein

Afford a present to the Infant God?

Hast thou no vers, no hymn, or solemn strein,

To welcom him to this his new abode,

Now while the Heav'n by the Suns team untrod,

Hath took no print of the approching light,

And all the spangled host keep watch in squadrons bright?

IV

See how from far upon the Eastern rode

The Star-led Wisards haste with odours sweet,

O run,prevent them with thy humble ode,

And lay it lowly at his blessed feet;

Have thou the honour first, thy Lord to greet,

And joyn thy voice unto the Angel Quire,

From out his secret Altar toucht with hallow'd fire.

The Hymn

I

It was the Winter wilde,
While the Heav'n-born-childe,
All meanly wrapt in the rude manger lies;
Nature in aw to him
Had doff't her gawdy trim,
With her great Master so to sympathize:
It was no season then for her
To wanton with the Sun her lusty Paramour.

II

Only with speeches fair
She woo'd the gentle Air
To hide her guilty front with innocent Snow,
And on her naked shame,
Pollute with sinfull blame,
The Saintly Vail of Maiden white to throw,
Confounded, that her Makers eyes
Should look so near upon her foul deformities.

III

But he her fears to cease,

Sent down the meek-eyd Peace,

She crown'd with Olive green, came softly sliding

Down through the turning sphear

His ready Harbinger,

With Turtle wing the amorous clouds dividing,

And waving wide her mirtle wand,

She strikes a universall Peace through Sea and Land.

IV

No War, or Battails sound

Was heard the World around,

The idle spear and shield were high up hung;

The hooked Chariot stood

Unstain'd with hostile blood,

The Trumpet spake not to the armed throng,

And Kings sate still with awfull eye,

As if they surely knew their sovran Lord was by.

V

But peacefull was the night
Wherin the Prince of light
His raign of peace upon the earth began:
The Windes with wonder whist,
Smoothly the waters kist,
Whispering new joyes to the milde Ocean,
Who now hath quite forgot to rave,
While Birds of Calm sit brooding on the charmed wave.

VI

The Stars with deep amaze
Stand fit in steadfast gaze,
Bending one way their pretious influence,
And will not take their flight,
For all the morning light,
Or Lucifer that often warned them thence;
But in their glimmering Orbs did glow,
Until their Lord himself bespake, and bid them go.

VII

And though the shady gloom

Had given day her room,

The Sun himself with-held his wonted speed,

And hid his head for shame,

As his inferior flame,

The new enlightened world no more should need;

He saw a greater Sun appear

Then his bright Throne, or burning Axletree could bear.

VIII

The Shepherds on the Lawn,

Or ere the point of dawn,

Sate simply chatting in a rustic row;

Full little thought they than,

That the mighty Pan

Was kindly com to live with them below;

Perhaps their loves, or els their sheep,

Was all that did their silly thoughts so busie keep.

IX

When such Musick sweet
Their hearts and ears did greet,
As never was by mortal finger strook,
Divinely-warbled voice
Answering the stringed noise,
As all their souls in blisfull rapture took:
The Air such pleasure loth to lose,
Withthousand echo's still prolongs each heav'nly close.

X

Nature that heard suchsound
Beneaththe hollow round
of Cynthia's seat the Airy region thrilling,
Now was almost won
To think her part was don
And that her raign had here its last fulfilling;
She knew such harmony alone
Could hold all Heav'n and Earth in happier union.

XI

At last surrounds their sight
A globe of circular light,
That with long beams the shame faced night arrayed
The helmed Cherubim
And sworded Seraphim,
Are seen in glittering ranks with wings displaid,
Harping in loud and solemn quire,
With unexpressive notes to Heav'ns new-born Heir.

XII

Such Musick (as 'tis said)
Before was never made,
But when of old the sons of morning sung,
While the Creator Great
His constellations set,
And the well-ballanc't world on hinges hung,
And cast the dark foundations deep,
And bid the weltring waves their oozy channel keep.

XIII

Ring out ye Crystall sphears,
Once bless our human ears,
(If ye have power to touch our senses so)
And let your silver chime
Move in melodious time;
And let the Base of Heav'ns deep Organ blow,
And with your ninefold harmony
Make up full consort to th'Angelike symphony.

XIV

For if such holy Song
Enwrap our fancy long,
Time will run back, and fetch the age of gold,
And speckl'd vanity
Will sicken soon and die,
And leprous sin will melt from earthly mould,
And Hell it self will pass away
And leave her dolorous mansions to the peering day.

XV

Yea Truth, and Justice then

Will down return to men,

Th'enameld Arras of the Rain-bow wearing,

And Mercy set between

Thron'd in Celestiall sheen,

With radiant feet the tissued clouds down stearing,

And Heav'n as at som festivall,

Will open wide the gates of her high Palace Hall.

XVI

But wisest Fate sayesno,

This must not yet be so,

The Babe lies yet in smiling Infancy,

That on the bitter cross

Must redeem our loss;

So both himself and us to glorifie:

Yet first to those ychain'd in sleep,

The Wakeful trump of doom must thunder through
  the deep,

XVII

With such a horrid clang
As on Mount Sinai rang
While the red fire, and smouldring clouds out brake:
The aged Earth agast
With terrour of that blast,
Shall from the surface to the center shake;
When at the worlds last session,
The dreadfull Judge in middle Air shall spread his throne.

XVIII

And then at lastour bliss
Full and perfect is,
But now begins; for from this happy day
Th'old Dragon under ground
In straiter limits bound,
Not half so far casts his usurped sway,
And wrath to see his Kingdom fail,
Swindges the scaly Horrour of his foulded tail.

XIX

The Oracles are dumm,

No voice or hideous humm

Runs through the arched roof in words deceiving.

Apollo from his shrine

Can no more divine,

With hollow shreik the steep of Delphos leaving.

No nightly trance, or breathed spell,

Inspire's the pale-ey'd Priest from the prophetic cell.

XX

The lonely mountains o're,

And the resounding shore,

A voice of weeping heard, and loud lament;

From haunted spring, and dale

Edg'd with poplar pale

The parting Genius is with sighing sent,

With flowre-inwov'n tresses torn

The Nimphs in twilight shade of tangled thickets mourn.

XXI

In consecrated Earth,

And on the holy Hearth,

The Lars, and Lemures moan with midnight plaint,

In Urns, and Altars round,

A drear, and dying sound

Affrights the Flamins at their service quaint;

And the chill Marble seems to sweat,

While each peculiar power forgoes his wonted seat.

XXII

Peor, and Baalim,

Forsake their Temples dim,

With that twise-batter'd god of Palestine,

And mooned Ashtaroth,

Heav'ns Queen and Mother both,

Now sits not girt with Tapers holy shine,

The Libyc Hammon shrinks his horn,

In vain the Tyrian Maids their wounded Thamuz mourn.

XXIII

And sullen Moloch fled,
Hath left in shadows dred,
His burning Idol all of blackest hue,
In vain with Cymbals ring,
They call the grisly king,
In dismall dance about the furnace Blue;
And Brutish gods of Nile as fast,
Isis and Orus, and the Dog Anubis hast.

XXIV

Nor is Osiris seen
In Memphian grove or green,
 Trampling the unshower'd grass with lowings loud;
Nor can he be at rest
Within his sacred chest,
 Naught but profoundest Hell can be his shroud:
In vain with timbrel'd anthems dark
The sable-stoled sorcerers bear his worshipp'd ark.

XXV

He feels from Juda's land
The dreaded Infant's hand,
    The rays of Bethlehem blind his dusky eyn;
Nor all the gods beside
Longer dare abide,
    Not Typhon huge ending in snaky twine:
Our Babe, to show his Godhead true,
Can in his swaddling bands control the damned crew.

XXVI

So when the Sun in bed,
Curtain'd with cloudy red,
    Pillows his chin upon an orient wave,
The flocking shadows pale
Troop to th'infernal jail,
    Each fetter'd ghost slips to his several grave,
And the yellow-skirted fays
Fly after the night-steeds, leaving their moon-lov'd maze.

XXVII

But see, the Virgin blest
Hath laid her Babe to rest:
    Time is our tedious song should here have ending.
Heav'n's youngest-teemed star,
Hath fix'd her polish'd car,
    Her sleeping Lord with handmaid lamp attending;
And all about the courtly stable,
Bright-harness'd Angels sit in order serviceable.

GOOD KING WENCESLAS

Translated from the Latin by J. M. Neale

Good King Wenceslas looked out
 On the Feast of Stephen,
When the snow lay round about,
 Deep, and crisp, and even.

Brightly shone the moon that night
 Though the frost was cruel,
When a poor man came in sight,
 Gath'ring winter fuel.

"Hither, page, and stand by me,
 If thou know'st it, telling.
Yonder peasant, who is he?
 Where and what his dwelling?"

"Sire, he lives a good league hence,
 Underneath the mountain;

Right against the forest fence,
    By Saint Agnes' fountain."

"Bring me flesh, and bring me wine,
    Bring me pine-logs hither;
Thou and I shall see him dine,
    When we bear them thither."

Page and monarch, forth they went,
    Forth they went together;
Through the rude wind's wild lament
    And the bitter weather.

"Sire, the night is darker now,
    And the wind blows stronger;
Fails my heart, I know not how,
    I can go no longer."

"Mark my footsteps, good my page;
    Tread thou in them boldly:
Thou shalt find the winter rage
    Freeze thy blood less coldly."

In his master's steps he trod,
    Where the snow lay dinted;

Heat was in the very sod
    Where the saint has printed.

Therefore, Christian men, be sure,
    Wealth or rank possessing,
Ye who now will bless the poor,
    Shall yourselves find blessing.

CHRISTMAS EVE CUSTOMS

An excerpt by Robert Herrick

Come, guard this night the Christmas-pie,
That the thief, though ne'er so sly,
With his flesh-hooks, don't come nigh
    To catch it.

From him, who alone sits there,
Having his eyes still in his ear,
And a deal of nightly fear
    To watch it.

OUR JOYFUL FEAST

George Wither

So, now is come our joyful feast,
    Let every soul be jolly!
Each room with ivy leaves is drest,
    And every post with holly.
Though some churls at our mirth repine,
Round your brows let garlands twine,
Drown sorrow in a cup of wine,
    And let us all be merry!

Now all our neighbours' chimneys smoke,
    And Christmas logs are burning;
Their ovens with baked meats do choke,
    And all their spits are turning.
Without the door let sorrow lie,
And if for cold it hap to die,
We'll bury it in Christmas pie,
    And evermore be merry!

THE BELLS

Excerpt by Edgar Allen Poe

Hear the sledges with the bells—
    Silver bells!
What a world of merriment their melody foretells!
    How they tinkle, tinkle, tinkle,
      In the icy air of night!
    While the stars, that oversprinkle
    All the heavens, seem to twinkle
      With a crystalline delight;
    Keeping time, time, time,
    In a sort if Runic rhyme,
To the tintinabulation that so musically wells
    From the bells, bells, bells, bells,
      Bells, bells, bells,—
From the jingling and the tinkling of the bells.

CHRISTMAS AT SEA

Robert Louis Stevenson

The sheets were frozen hard, and they cut the naked
hand;

The decks were like a slide, where a seaman scarce
could stand;

The wind was a nor'wester, blowing squally off the
sea;

And cliffs and spouting breakers were the only
things a-lee.

They heard the surf a-roaring before the break of
day;

But 'twas only with the peep of light we saw how ill
we lay.

We tumbled every hand on deck instanter, with a
shout,

And we gave her the maintops'l, and stood by to go
about.

All day we tacked and tacked between the South
  Head and the North;
All day we hauled the frozen sheets, and got no
  further forth;
All day as cold as charity, in bitter pain and dread,
For very life and nature, we tacked from head to head.

We gave the South a wider berth, for there the tide-
  race roared;
But every tack we made we brought the North Head
  close aboard;
So's we saw the cliffs and houses, and the breakers
  running high,
And the coast-guard in his garden, with his glass
  against his eye.

The frost was on the village roofs as white as ocean
  foam;
The good red fires were burning bright in every
  'longshore home;
The windows sparkled clear, and the chimneys
  volleyed out;
And I vow we sniffed the victuals as the vessel went
  about.

The bells upon the church were rung with a mighty
  jovial cheer;
For it's just that I should tell you how (of all days in the
  year)
This day of our adversity was blessed Christmas morn,
And the house above the coast-guard's was the house
  where I was born.

Oh, well I saw the pleasant room, the pleasant faces
  there,
My mother's silver spectacles, my father's silver hair;
And well I saw the firelight, like a flight of homely
  elves,
Go dancing round the china plates that stand upon
  the shelves.

And well I knew the talk they had, the talk that was of
  me,
Of the shadow on the household, and the son that
  went to sea;
And, oh, the wicked fool I seemed, in every kind of
  way,
To be here and hauling frozen ropes on blessed
  Christmas Day.

They lit the high sea-light, and the dark began to fall.
"All hands to loose topgallant sails!" I heard the
  captain call.
"By the Lord, she'll never stand it," our first mate,
  Jackson, cried.
"It's the one way or the other, Mr. Jackson," he
  replied.

She staggered to her bearings, but the sails were new
  and good,
And the ship smelt up to windward just as though she
  understood.
As the winter's day was ending, in the entry of the
  night,
We cleared the weary headland, and passed below
  the light.

And they heaved a mighty breath, every soul on
  board but me,
As they saw her nose again pointing handsome out to
  sea;
But all that I could think of, in the darkness and the
  cold,
Was just that I was leaving home and my folks were
  growing old.

CHRISTMAS IN THE OLDEN TIME

Sir Walter Scott

The damsel donned her kirtle sheen;
The hall was dressed with holly green;
Forth to the wood did merry-men go
To gather in the mistletoe.
Then opened wide the baron's hall
To vassal, tenant, serf, and all;
Power laid his rod of rule aside,
And ceremony doffed his pride.
The heir, with roses in his shoes,
That night might village partner choose;
The lord underogating share
The vulgar game of post-and-pair.
All hailed with uncontrolled delight
And general voice, the happy night,
That to the cottage as the crown
Brought tidings of salvation down.

The fire with well-dried logs supplied
Went roaring up the chimney wide;
The huge hall-table's oaken face,
Scrubbed till it shone, the day to grace,
Bore then upon its massive board
No mark to part the squire and lord.
Then was brought in the lusty brawn
By old blue-coated serving-man;
Then the grim boar's head frowned on high,
Crested with bay and rosemary.
Well can the green-garbed ranger tell
How, when, and where the monster fell;
What dogs before his death he tore,
And all the baiting of the boar.
The wassail round, in good brown bowls,
Garnished with ribbons blithely trowls.
There the huge sirloin reeked; hard by
Plum-porridge stood and Christmas-pie;
Nor failed old Scotland to produce
At such high tide her savory goose.
Then came the merry masquers in
And carols roared with blithesome din;
If unmelodious was the song,
It was a hearty note and strong.

Who lists may in their mumming see
Traces of ancient mystery.
While shirts supplied the masquerade,
And smutted cheeks the visors made:
But, oh! what masquers richly dight
Can boast of bosoms half so light!
England was merry England when
Old Christmas brought his sports again.
'Twas Christmas broached the mightiest ale,
'Twas Christmas told the merriest tale;
A Christmas gambol oft would cheer
The poor man's heart through half the year.

A PATCH OF OLD SNOW

Robert Frost

There's a patch of old snow in a corner
    That I should have guessed
Was a blow-away paper the rain
    Had brought to rest.

It is speckled with grime as if
    Small print overspread it,
The news of a day I've forgotten—
    If I ever read it.

A VISIT FROM ST. NICHOLAS

Clement C. Moore

'Twas the night before Christmas, when all through
  the house
Not a creature was stirring, not even a mouse;
The stockings were hung by the chimney with care
In hopes that St. Nicholas soon would be there;

The children were nestled all snug in their beds,
While visions of sugar-plums danced in their heads;
And mamma in her kerchief, and I in my cap,
Had just settled our brains for a long winter's nap,

Then out on the lawn there arose such a clatter,
I sprang from the bed to see what was the matter.
Away to the window I flew like a flash,
Tore open the shutters and threw up the sash.

The moon on the breast of the new-fallen snow
Gave the lustre of mid-day to objects below,
When, what to my wondering eyes should appear,
But a miniature sleigh, and eight tiny reindeer,

W ith a little old driver, so lively and quick,
I knew in a moment it must be St. Nick.
More rapid than eagles his coursers they came,
And he whistled, and shouted, and called them by name:

Now, Dasher! now, Dancer! now, Prancer and Vixen!
On, Comet! on, Cupid! on, Donder and Blitzen!
To the top of the porch! to the top of the wall!
Now dash away! dash away! dash away all!"

A s dry leaves that before the wild hurricane fly,
When they meet with an obstacle, mount to the sky;
So up to the house-top the coursers they flew,
With the sleigh full of Toys, and St. Nicholas too.

And then, in a twinkling, I heard on the roof
The prancing and pawing of each little hoof.
As I drew in my head, and was turning around,
Down the chimney St. Nicholas came with a bound.

H e was dressed all in fur, from his head to his foot,
And his clothes were all tarnished with ashes and soot;
A bundle of Toys he had flung on his back,
And he looked like a peddler just opening his pack.

His eyes—how they twinkled! his dimples how merry!
His cheeks were like roses, his nose like a cherry!
His droll little mouth was drawn up like a bow,
And the beard of his chin was as white as the snow;

The stump of a pipe he held tight in his teeth,
And the smoke it encircled his head like a wreath;
He had a broad face and a little round belly,
That shook when he laughed, like a bowlful of jelly.

He was chubby and plump, a right jolly old elf,
And I laughed when I saw him, in spite of myself;
A wink of his eye and a twist of his head,
Soon gave me to know I had nothing to dread;

He spoke not a word, but went straight to his work,
And filled all the stockings; then turned with a jerk,
And laying his finger aside of his nose,
And giving a nod, up the chimney he rose;

He sprang to his sleigh, to his team gave a whistle,

And away they all flew like the down of a thistle.

But I heard him exclaim, ere he drove out of sight,

"Happy Christmas to all, and to all a good-night."

TO MRS. K., ON HER SENDING ME ENGLISH CHRISTMAS PLUMB-CAKE, AT PARIS

Helen Maria Williams

What crowding thoughts around me wake,
  What marvels in a Christmas-cake!
Ah say, what strange enchantment dwells
  Enclos'd within its od'rous cells?
Is there no small magician bound
  Encrusted in its snowy round?
For magic surely lurks in this,
  A cake that tells of vanish'd bliss;
A cake that conjures up to view
  The early scenes, when life was new;
When mem'ry knew no sorrows past,
  And hope believ'd in joys that last! —
Mysterious cake, whose folds contain

Life's calendar of bliss and pain;
That speaks of friends for ever fled,
And wakes the tears I love to shed.
Oft shall I breathe her cherish'd name
From whose fair hand the off'ring came:
For she recalls the artless smile
Of nymphs that deck my native Isle;
Of beauty that we love to trace,
Allied with tender, modest grace;
Of those who, while abroad they roam,
Retain each charm that gladdens home,
And whose dear friendship can impart
A Christmas banquet for the heart!

(Courtesy of www.eighteenthcenturypoetry.org)

CHRISTMAS TREES

Robert Frost

The city had withdrawn into itself
And left at last the country to the country;
When between whirls of snow not come to lie
And whirls of foliage not yet laid, there drove
A stranger to our yard, who looked the city,
Yet did in country fashion in that there
He sat and waited till he drew us out
A-buttoning coats to ask him who he was.
He proved to be the city come again
To look for something it had left behind
And could not do without and keep its Christmas.
He asked if I would sell my Christmas trees;
My woods—the young fir balsams like a place
Where houses all are churches and have spires.
I hadn't thought of them as Christmas Trees.
I doubt if I was tempted for a moment

To sell them off their feet to go in cars
And leave the slope behind the house all bare,
Where the sun shines now no warmer than the moon.
I'd hate to have them know it if I was.
Yet more I'd hate to hold my trees except
As others hold theirs or refuse for them,
Beyond the time of profitable growth,
The trial by market everything must come to.
I dallied so much with the thought of selling.
Then whether from mistaken courtesy
And fear of seeming short of speech, or whether
From hope of hearing good of what was mine,
I said, "There aren't enough to be worth while."
"I could soon tell how many they would cut,
You let me look them over."

"You could look.
But don't expect I'm going to let you have them."
Pasture they spring in, some in clumps too close
That lop each other of boughs, but not a few
Quite solitary and having equal boughs
All round and round. The latter he nodded "Yes" to,
Or paused to say beneath some lovelier one,

With a buyer's moderation, "That would do."
I thought so too, but wasn't there to say so.
We climbed the pasture on the south, crossed over,
And came down on the north.

                                        He said, "A thousand."

"A thousand Christmas trees!—at what apiece?"

He felt some need of softening that to me:
"A thousand trees would come to thirty dollars."

Then I was certain I had never meant
To let him have them. Never show surprise!
But thirty dollars seemed so small beside
The extent of pasture I should strip, three cents
(For that was all they figured out apiece),
Three cents so small beside the dollar friends
I should be writing to within the hour
Would pay in cities for good trees like those,
Regular vestry-trees whole Sunday Schools
Could hang enough on to pick off enough.
A thousand Christmas trees I didn't know I had!
Worth three cents more to give away than sell,

As may be shown by a simple calculation.
Too bad I couldn't lay one in a letter.
I can't help wishing I could send you one,
In wishing you herewith a Merry Christmas.

MISTLETOE

Walter de la Mare

———————

Sitting under the mistletoe
(Pale-green, fairy mistletoe),
One last candle burning low,
All the sleepy dancers gone,
Just one candle burning on,
Shadows lurking everywhere:
Some one came, and kissed me there.

Tired I was; my head would go
Nodding under the mistletoe
(Pale-green, fairy mistletoe),
No footsteps came, no voice, but only,
Just as I sat there, sleepy, lonely,
Stooped in the still and shadowy air
Lips unseen and kissed me there.

(Courtesy of WikiSource)

THE MAGI

William Butler Yeats

Now as at all times I can see in the mind's eye,
In their stiff, painted clothes, the pale unsatisfied ones
Appear and disappear in the blue depth of the sky
With all their ancient faces like rain-beaten stones,
And all their helms of silver hovering side by side,
And all their eyes still fixed, hoping to find once more,
Being by Calvary's turbulence unsatisfied,
The uncontrollable mystery on the bestial floor.

(Courtesy of WikiSource)

LITTLE TREE

E. E. Cummings

little tree
little silent Christmas tree
you are so little
you are more like a flower

who found you in the green forest
and were you very sorry to come away?
seei will comfort you
because you smell so sweetly

i will kiss your cool bark
and hug you safe and tight
just as your mother would,
only don't be afraid

lookthe spangles
that sleep all the year in a dark box

dreaming of being taken out and allowed to
shine,
the balls the chains red and gold the fluffy
threads,

put up your little arms
and i'll give them all to you to hold.
every finger shall have its ring
and there won't be a single place dark or
unhappy

then when you're quite dressed
you'll stand in the window for everyone to see
and how they'll stare!
oh but you'll be very proud

and my little sister and i will take hands
and looking up at our beautiful tree
we'll dance and sing
"Noel Noel"

(Courtesy of WikiSource)

WINTER-TIME

Robert Louis Stevenson

Late lies the wintry sun a-bed,
A frosty, fiery sleepy-head;
Blinks but an hour or two; and then,
A blood-red orange, sets again.

Before the stars have left the skies,
At morning in the dark I rise;
And shivering in my nakedness,
By the cold candle, bathe and dress.

Close by the jolly fire I sit
To warm my frozen bones a bit;
Or with a reindeer-sled, explore
The colder countries round the door.

When to go out, my nurse doth wrap
Me in my comforter and cap;

The cold wind burns my face and blows
Its frosty pepper up my nose.

Black are my steps on silver sod;
Thick blows my frosty breath abroad;
And tree and house, and hill and lake,
Are frosted like a wedding-cake.

MUSIC ON CHRISTMAS MORNING

Anne Brontë

Music I love—but never strain
Could kindle raptures so divine,
So grief assuage, so conquer pain,
And rouse this pensive heart of mine—
As that we hear on Christmas morn,
Upon the wintry breezes borne.

Though Darkness still her empire keep,
And hours must pass, ere morning break;
From troubled dreams, or slumbers deep,
That music KINDLY bids us wake:
It calls us, with an angel's voice,
To wake, and worship, and rejoice;

To greet with joy the glorious morn,

Which angels welcomed long ago,
When our redeeming Lord was born,
To bring the light of Heaven below;
The Powers of Darkness to dispel,
And rescue Earth from Death and Hell.

While listening to that sacred strain,
My raptured spirit soars on high;
I seem to hear those songs again
Resounding through the open sky,
That kindled such divine delight,
In those who watched their flocks by night.

With them I celebrate His birth—
Glory to God, in highest Heaven,
Good-will to men, and peace on earth,
To us a Saviour-king is given;
Our God is come to claim His own,
And Satan's power is overthrown!

A sinless God, for sinful men,
Descends to suffer and to bleed;
Hell MUST renounce its empire then;
The price is paid, the world is freed,

And Satan's self must now confess
That Christ has earned a RIGHT to bless:

Now holy Peace may smile from heaven,
And heavenly Truth from earth shall spring:
The captive's galling bonds are riven,
For our Redeemer is our king;
And He that gave his blood for men
Will lead us home to God again.

THE HOUSE OF CHRISTMAS

G. K. Chesterton

There fared a mother driven forth
Out of an inn to roam;
In the place where she was homeless
All men are at home.
The crazy stable close at hand,
With shaking timber and shifting sand,
Grew a stronger thing to abide and stand
Than the square stones of Rome.

For men are homesick in their homes,
And strangers under the sun,
And they lay their heads in a foreign land
Whenever the day is done.
Here we have battle and blazing eyes,
And chance and honour and high surprise,
Where the yule tale was begun.

A Child in a foul stable,
Where the beasts feed and foam;
Only where He was homeless
Are you and I at home;
We have hands that fashion and heads that
But our hearts we lost—how long ago!
In a place no chart nor ship can show
Under the sky's dome.

This world is wild as an old wives' tale,
And strange the plain things are,
The earth is enough and the air is enough
For our wonder and our war;
But our rest is as far as the fire-drake swings
And our peace is put in impossible things
Where clashed and thundered unthinkable wings
Round an incredible star.

To an open house in the evening
Home shall men come,
To an older place than Eden
And a taller town than Rome.
To the end of the way of the wandering star,
To the things that cannot be and that are,

To the place where God was homeless
And all men are at home.

BEFORE THE ICE IS IN THE POOLS (XLV.)

Emily Dickinson

―――――――――

Before the ice is in the pools,
  Before the skaters go,
Or any cheek at nightfall
  Is tarnished by the snow,

Before the fields have finished,
  Before the Christmas tree,
Wonder upon wonder
  Will arrive to me!

What we touch the hems of
  On a summer's day;
What is only walking
  Just a bridge away;

That which sings so, speaks so,
  When there's no one here, —
Will the frock I wept in
  Answer me to wear?

RING OUT, WILD BELLS

Alfred, Lord Tennyson

———————

Ring out, wild bells, to the wild sky,
The flying cloud, the frosty light:
The year is dying in the night;
Ring out, wild bells, and let him die.

Ring out the old, ring in the new,
Ring, happy bells, across the snow:
The year is going, let him go;
Ring out the false, ring in the true.

Ring out the grief that saps the mind,
For those that here we see no more;
Ring out the feud of rich and poor,
Ring in redress to all mankind.

Ring out a slowly dying cause,
And ancient forms of party strife;
Ring in the nobler modes of life,
With sweeter manners, purer laws.

Ring out the want, the care, the sin,
The faithless coldness of the times;
Ring out, ring out my mournful rhymes,
But ring the fuller minstrel in.

Ring out false pride in place and blood,
The civic slander and the spite;
Ring in the love of truth and right,
Ring in the common love of good.

Ring out old shapes of foul disease;
Ring out the narrowing lust of gold;
Ring out the thousand wars of old,
Ring in the thousand years of peace.

Ring in the valiant man and free,
The larger heart, the kindlier hand;
Ring out the darkness of the land,
Ring in the Christ that is to be.

(Courtesy of WikiSource)

ABOUT BUSHEL & PECK BOOKS

Bushel & Peck Books is a children's publishing house with a special mission. Through our Book-for-Book Promise™, we donate one book to kids in need for every book we sell. Our beautiful books are given to kids through schools, libraries, local neighborhoods, shelters, nonprofits, and also to many selfless organizations that are working hard to make a difference. So thank you for purchasing this book! Because of you, another book will make its way into the hands of a child who needs it most.

NOMINATE A SCHOOL OR ORGANIZATION TO RECEIVE FREE BOOKS

Do you know a school, library, or organization that could use some free books for their kids? We'd love to help! Please fill out the nomination form on our website (see below), and we'll do everything we can to make something happen.

www.bushelandpeckbooks.com/pages/
nominate-a-school-or-organization

If you liked this book, please leave a review online at your favorite retailer. Honest reviews spread the word about Bushel & Peck—and help us make better books, too!

Printed in the United States
by Baker & Taylor Publisher Services